Soap Making:How to make Soap:

The Essential Soap Making Guide for Beginners (34 Incredible DIY Homemade Natural Soap Recipes)

I want to thank you and congratulate you for downloading the book, *"Soap Making:How to make Soap: The Essential Soap Making Guide for Beginners (34 Incredible DIY Homemade Natural Soap Recipes)"*.

This book contains information on how to make your own homemade natural soaps.

Making your own soap is not difficult to do. At first, you will need to familiarize yourself with the different ingredients that typically go with soap making. You need to exercise necessary precaution in handling some of the ingredients. You also need to make sure to wear the right gear when preparing your soap.

In creating your own soap, you have the freedom to choose the ingredients for your recipe. You can create your own unique blend that can never be found anywhere in the world.

You can have your soap for personal use, give your homemade soaps as gifts for birthdays and the holidays, and/or make some profit by selling them.

As time goes by, you will be able to concoct your own blend without having to look at the recipes from this book. Soap making is a worthwhile hobby that you will enjoy doing again and again.

Thanks again for downloading this book, I hope you enjoy it!

Chapter 1: Making your Own Soap

Soap making is a worthwhile hobby that you can also convert into a home-based business that can help you improve your financial standing or give you an added source of income. Some make personalized soaps to give as gifts. They use the favorite scent and/or ingredient of the receiver in making the soap.

You can also make soaps for the whole family. These homemade natural soaps are practical, economical, and safe.

Benefits of Making your Own Soaps

Although commercial soaps were made to clean your skin, they can also potentially harm you. Different soap manufacturers might use chemicals in producing their soaps, and these same chemicals could harm your body in the long run.

Soap is produced from a chemical reaction made possible by mixing lye, water, and oils. The chemical reaction is known as saponification. During the process (stirring), the lye helps form the soap. You need to stir until it thickens, and when it does, you can pour the mixture into the mold. Otherwise, you will have an incomplete reaction that could lead to partial separation of fat and lye solution.

If you make your own soap, then you can choose the ingredients that should go well with your soap. You can make a "safe" soap that you and your family can use every day. You don't need to worry about any harmful chemical penetrating your skin.

It is economical and practical to produce your own soap. You can mass produce your soap and store it in a dry place. You don't need to worry about rushing to a grocery store ever again just because you run out of soap. You can always replenish your stock the moment you see that you only have two to three bars left.

You get to choose the fragrance of your soap or how strong the scent should be. You can also opt not to include any fragrance at all, especially if you have a sensitive nose.

Natural homemade soaps let you retain full glycerin in your soap. Glycerin can help keep the skin moisturized. Most commercially produced soaps lack glycerin. Soap manufacturers usually mine the glycerin from the finished soaps and sell it separately at a higher price

The Different Types of Soap

There are different types of soap and you can make each type by yourself with some help from this book. Take a look at the different types of soap and see which one tickles your fancy. Try one type first and try the rest later when you feel like doing more.

Beauty and Perfumed Soaps

Beauty and perfumed soaps are popular among women. These soaps come in a variety of scents and ingredients that target specific skin problem while cleaning the skin and getting rid of impurities that can cause further harm.

Most women love to pamper their skin and prefer to get a soap that can give them everything they want for their skin while being embraced in the scent they want to wear.

Novelty Soaps

Novelty soaps usually come in different shapes and sizes that intend not only to clean, but give delight to the user. These soaps may also come in different colors and serve as decorative pieces.

To make the younger children in the house wash their hands without being told, you can make a novelty soap that shaped like a crayon, animal, or any of their favorite toy. There are several soap molds that you can choose from and all you need is choose the one they will like best.

Guest Soaps

Guest soaps often come in miniature sizes and possess attractive shapes. If the homeowner wants to leave a lasting impression on her guests, she makes sure that everything is perfect, including the soap that her guests will use.

Some choose simple designs while there are others who choose fancy designs for their guest soaps.

Laundry Soaps

Laundry soaps are especially formulated to wipe out dirt, grease, organic compounds, and particles that got trapped within the fabric of your clothes. But, there are also delicate fabrics that need gentle laundry soap to wash them. In choosing the laundry soap to use, make sure to take into consideration the kind of fabric that you need to clean.

Kitchen Soaps

There are two categories of kitchen soaps: dish soap and cleansers. Reliable dish soaps or detergents can cut through tough grease and dirt to give you sparkling clean dishes and drinking glasses.

Cleansers can help clean your kitchen surface most especially if there is tough grease, debris, or stain that needs good wiping. It is prudent to use the cleanser with mild abrasive.

Medicated Soaps

A medicated soap is also called germicidal or anti-bacterial soap. It has antiseptics and can disinfect a wound. Unfortunately, there are medicated soaps being sold in stores that only intend to lure customers to buy them and offer no benefit at all other than being able to clean wounds.

Understand that this book aims to guide a complete beginner, and it is prudent to start with uncomplicated methods and simple ingredients. There are some sections that give the reader a sort of overview of other things to expect in making soap.

To complete the basics, you need to learn about the ingredients, the tools to use, and the usual process in soap making. You will find all of these in the succeeding chapters.

Chapter 2: Getting to Know your Ingredients

The ingredients presented in this chapter are the basic or typical ingredients that you need for producing soaps. There are recipes that might require you to add something else aside from the ingredients that you will learn in this chapter.

Lye (Sodium Hydroxide or Caustic Soda)

It is true that you cannot make your own soap without lye. You will find recipes using soap base instead of lye, but know that the soap base was created with lye.

When using lye, it is recommended to use 100% sodium hydroxide or the crystal form of lye. You need to wear gloves, mask, and goggles when handling lye to avoid accidents.

Lye can burn your skin and leave holes in fabric—thus, you need to be extra careful when working with lye. When mixed in water, lye will heat up and emit fumes which can choke you. However, the whole thing usually lasts only for a minute.

It is advisable to add lye to the water and not the other way around. You also need to stir right away because it could explode when you allow it to clump. It is also good to know that lye disappears when the mixture has undergone saponification. When that happens, you need not worry because your finished soap is lye free.

Consider these when handling lye:

- You should not let lye touch your skin because it might burn your skin.
- Wear gloves, goggles, a mask, and an apron when preparing your lye solution.
- Make sure that your work area is well-ventilated (Work outside your home if you must.) to avoid inhaling fumes.

Soap Base

Soap base is the most typical ingredient in any melt and pour natural soap. Soap base is usually clear. There are vendors who offer opaque or white colored soap base (a colorant was already added).

Water (or Other Liquids)

Water (and/or other liquids like goat milk) is important during saponification. However, you won't see any trace of liquid when you begin using your finished soap. Water or other liquids will evaporate during the curing period and leave your bars a bit smaller and harder.

Oils

You can use any oil or fat in creating your own blend of soap. You can actually use up to a dozen oil types, but it is recommended to stick to using two to five oils. Each type of soap may yield a certain characteristic that is inherent to the oil that was used to produce the soap.

Some of the oil or fat that you can use are cocoa butter, coconut oil, beeswax, palm oil, Shea butter, olive oil, soybean oil, and sweet almond oil.

Fragrance

You may or may not use fragrance in your soap – depends on your preference or mood. Fragrance oil or essential oil is commonly added to the soap mixture when you want a fragrant soap. You only need to choose the scent that you want.

Do not use candle or craft fragrance and potpourri in making soap.

Colorants

Natural colorants are sometimes added to make the soaps attractive. Some soap makers use cosmetic clays that usually come in pink (almost red), white, and green. Clay can also help exfoliate the skin.

There are some who prefer to use mineral and mica powders due to their wide assortment of colors.

Herbs

If you want to include herb, then use dried herbs. Soap makers love to include lavender, rosemary, and chamomile.

These ingredients are the basic ingredients in making soap. As you become an expert in soap making, you might encounter other ingredients that you want to include. Just make sure that your chosen ingredients won't adversely react to any of the ingredients that you already have.

Chapter 3: Your Tools and Other Essentials

Soap making is something fun to do, although it may require a bit of patience on your part. It also helps a lot if you have all the tools and other essentials that you will need in creating your natural soap.

Pot

Stainless steel pot is recommended for soap making. The lye reacts to aluminum, cast iron, or Teflon-coated pot and it is wise to stay away from such pots. A pot that's enamel-covered could be a good choice too. However, if you are working using stick blender then it is possible that the enamel might accidentally chip off.

Bowls

You will also need different bowls for mixing your soap. Make sure that you have a stainless bowl or Pyrex so you don't have to deal with issues regarding the heat. You can use glass, stainless, or plastic for your spoons and bowls. When using plastic material, see to it that it won't melt when you need to mix some hot ingredients in it. It is also advisable to stay away from wood or aluminum bowls.

Stick Blender

A stick blender or immersion blender can cut your preparation time in half (or more). It also gives better result than normal manual stirring. An hour's worth of mixing and blending the ingredients together can be accomplished in five minutes. Choose something durable (though a bit pricey) that will be able to render its service for a long time.

Measuring Cups and Spoons

Always choose stainless measuring spoons and cups when making your soap. Please refrain from using aluminum or wooden spoon and cup when making soaps.

Digital Scale

A digital scale helps you achieve precise measurement of the needed ingredients especially if you plan to work in small batches. You will also find a digital scale helpful around the kitchen.

Thermometer

You need this to determine the temperature of your mixture should the recipe call for one.

Freezer Paper

You will need this to serve as liner for your mold. The liner will prevent the soap from sticking to the mold.

Soap Mold

It is recommended to use a plastic or wood box as a mold for your soap. There are people who use cardboard box, but if you need something that can last long then get yourself a wood or plastic soap mold.

Knife or Soap Cutter

You can buy a soap cutter if you want or you can use your kitchen knife to cut your soap into bars.

Towels

You will need towels to wipe your work area or your hands.

Cardboard Box

Prepare a cardboard box that is big enough to accommodate your soap mold.

Gloves, Protective Glasses (or Goggles), Mask, and Apron

Since lye is caustic, you need to be careful in handling it. Wear gloves, protective glasses, mask, and apron every time you need to deal with such ingredients.

Newspaper or Vinyl Cover

You will need newspaper or vinyl cover to line your work area and protect your table or work area from stain or unsightly markings.

These are the basic things that you will need when working with your soap. Feel free to add some more if they would help you work much faster.

Chapter 4: Take a Peek on the Different Methods

There are different types of soap and there are different methods to prepare the soaps.

Cold Process

This method starts with liquefying the base oil/s together. Lye solution is then added to the mixture. Take note that the lye solution and oil mixture must have the same temperature (around 90°F or according to recipe) before combining them.

Modern soap makers, however, found out that 20°F is perfect for making soap, and the oils and lye solution only need to reach that temperature range – having the same temperature is no longer a requirement.

The oil and lye mixture must be blended using a whisk, or you can also use a stick blender until the mixture becomes thick. You can now pour the mixture into the soap mold that you have prepared.

You will need a stainless pan to melt the base oils, and a thermometer to help you determine the temperature of the mixture. You need to cure it for at least four weeks up to a maximum of six weeks before you can use the soap.

Room Temperature Method

This method is fast becoming the favorite among makers of natural soaps. You don't need a thermometer with this method. If you are using hard oils, make sure to melt it first (at room temperature) before adding the soft oils.

You can start preparing the lye solution by adding the required amount of lye to the required amount of water or liquid. Pour the solution onto the base oils. Stir everything gently.

Blend the mixture thoroughly until it is thick. Pour the thickened mixture into your choice of soap molds. Cure it for at least four weeks to six weeks. After that, you can now use the soap.

Hot Process

A number of soap makers prefer this method because it expedites the hardening of finished soaps. Many natural soap producers who make some profit from producing homemade soaps find this method the most advantageous.

This method requires melting of soft and hard oils together over low heat, and then adding the lye solution to the mixture. You don't need to check for the temperature of the lye solution and oil mixture.

Blend everything together until the mixture becomes thick. Cook the soap mixture until it resembles the consistency of the mashed potatoes. It should be somewhat translucent.

Scoop the mixture and put it into the soap mold and let it cool. Expect the appearance of the soap to be a bit rustic as compared to the other methods.

Applying Oven Process Method

You can use this oven process to any of the mentioned methods above. This can help speed up the curing (or eliminate the curing stage).

If you want to use room temperature or cold process method, then you need to cook the soap in the oven at 150°F to 170°F after pouring the mixture into the mold. Make sure to use oven safe soap molds. Cook until the mixture reached the gel stage.

Other soap makers would leave the molded soap in the hot oven after turning it off. They usually leave the soap in the oven overnight. There are others who prefer to cook it for a couple of hours before turning the oven off.

If you use hot process, then you can use the oven as your heat source for turning the soap mixture into something that resembles mashed potatoes. Others also use a double boiler or crock pot.

Whipped Soap Method

This method does not require you to apply heat to melt your oils – you don't need the oils to melt at all. If you use this method, then you need to chill the lye solution. The oil won't melt if the lye is chilled.

Whipped soap recipes are high in hard oils and may only contain minimal amounts of liquid oils. You need to whip the hard oils first until fluffy and creamy. You add the liquid oils to the whipped mixture, and blend well.

Make sure that the mixture of oils becomes fluffy before adding (slowly) the chilled lye solution. The mixture should turn thick and creamy.

Pour the mixture into the soap molds or you can also pipe it like icing onto butcher's paper. Create different designs. One good thing about whipped soaps is that they float.

Melt and Pour Method

Melt and pour method makes use of a soap base that has been prepared and made – you don't need to prepare the lye solution because it's already included in the soap base.

You only need to cut the soap base into smaller pieces, melt the pieces, and add your favorite color and fragrance (if you want one with scent). Mix everything well, and pour the melted mixture into your favorite soap mold.

You can use the soap once it has cooled and become firm to the touch.

In concocting your own recipe you can choose the method that you think is the most suitable for your recipe.

Chapter 5: The Usual Process and Finish

This chapter intends to take you on a short journey on the process of making soap and gives you an idea on how it's made.

After preparing your work area (newspaper or vinyl cover is lined on table), gather the things that you will need (tools and ingredients).

Put on your gloves, mask, goggles, and apron and begin measuring your ingredients.

Follow the method (see Chapter 4) that the recipe requires. If you are concocting your own blend, choose the most suitable method to use for your recipe.

If you are using lye, heed the warning that this book provided and stay safe.

To cool down the solution or mixture, put the bowl in a basin of cold water. You don't need to get the exact temperature, just make sure that the temperature of the solution or mixture is anywhere within the range of the suggested temperature in the recipe.

It is best to use a stick blender when mixing or blending your ingredients. Do not raise the blender to avoid stirring in air that might create bubbles or air pockets in your soap.

You can alternate blending and stirring if you want until the mixture resembles that of a pancake batter. Expect the mixture to turn dull and thinly coat the spoon.

You can now add colorants and fragrances if you want.

Pour the soap mixture in your soap mold before it cools down and becomes too thick.

This is what most soap makers do (if you are not following the oven process method): put the soap mold inside the cardboard box, and cover it with the lid. Cover the cardboard box with towel to keep it extra warm, you can skip this if you want.

You can clean your area by this time and wash the tools that you used.

The Finishing

After about 30 minutes, you can take a peek and check your soap. If you find a big crack on the middle, you can take off the towel to reduce temperature. Press the edges back down, gently, using your fingers.

The soap is usually dark and shiny in the center, and opaque on the edges. Just keep the soap inside the box.

After an hour, the soap should start to harden. You might need to keep the soap inside the box overnight.

When the soap turned hard and opaque all over, it is time to cut it into bars. Just lift it gently from the mold and peel off the lining. Use a knife to mark where you want to cut the soap.

Some soap makers fix the uneven or crooked cut by using a peeler, but if you don't want some parts of the soap go to waste then leave it as it is.

You can line your soap bars in the box where they can dry and age. The cardboard box can safeguard them from draft. It should not be air tight.

You can use the soap right away when it hardened all throughout. There are soap makers who prefer to wait at least 4 weeks before using their soaps just to make sure that the bars aged beautifully.

Chapter 6: Beauty Soap Recipes

Now the fun part begins (Always refer to Chapter 5 for guidance.).

1. Simple Olive Oil Soap

What you need:

2.5 ounces lye

7.5 ounces water

20 ounces olive oil

What to do:

1. Prepare everything that you will need – tools, ingredients, and protective gear. Always wear your protective gear prior to your ingredient preparation.

2. Put the water in a jug, and place it in the sink.

3. Make sure that the room is well-ventilated. Gently add lye in the water, and mix it using a long-stemmed spoon. Expect the solution to get hot; you need to be real careful when handling lye.

4. Leave the jug in the sink, and prepare your oil.

5. Get your stainless pan and heat the olive oil or base oil over low fire. Aim for 110°F. Turn off the heat.

6. Test the temperature of the lye solution if it's anywhere near the temperature of the oil.

7. Slowly add the lye solution to the oil, and carefully mix them together using your stick blender until the mixture resembles creamy custard.

8. Pour the mixture into the lined mold. Keep the soap mold in a cardboard box, and let it dry completely (see Chapter 5 "The Finishing").

2. Citrusy Tea Tree Oil Soap

What you need:

2.5 ounces lye

7.5 ounces water

20 ounces olive oil

15 drops orange essential oil

10 drops tea tree

What to do:

Do process 1 to 7 of "Simple Olive Oil Soap"

Add the essential oils and proceed with process 8 of "Simple Olive Oil Soap".

3. Relaxing Lavender Soap

What you need:

2.5 ounces lye

7.5 ounces water

20 ounces olive oil

30 drops lavender essential oil

2 tablespoons dried lavender heads, crushed

What to do:

Do steps 1 to 7 of "Simple Olive Oil Soap"

Add the essential oil and dried herb. Proceed with process 8 of "Simple Olive Oil Soap".

4. A Sweet, Sweet Blend

What you need:

2.5 ounces lye

7.5 ounces water

20 ounces olive oil

12 drops Ylang-ylang essential oil

10 drops each of Patchouli and Chamomile essential oil

2 tablespoons dried chamomile heads, crushed

What to do:

Do 1 to 7 of "Simple Olive Oil Soap" process.

Add the required amount of each essential oils followed by the dried herb.

Do process 8 of "Simple Olive Oil Soap".

5. Orange Rose Soap

This soap is great for acne.

What you need:

2.5 ounces lye

7.5 ounces water

20 ounces olive oil

18 drops rose essential oil

12 drops orange essential oil

1 tablespoon orange zest (optional), grated

1 tablespoon dried rose petals, slightly crushed

What to do:

Refer to steps 1 to 7 of "Simple Olive Oil Soap" process.

Add the essential oils, orange zest, and dried petals. Proceed to step 8 of "Simple Olive Oil Soap".

6. Hand and Body Beauty Bar

What you need:

2.5 ounces lye

7.5 ounces water

10 ounces coconut oil

10 ounces olive oil

20 drops grape seed essential oil

12 drops almond essential oil

What to do:

See steps 1 to 7 of "Simple Olive Oil Soap".

Add the essential oils, and proceed to step 8 of "Simple Olive Oil Soap".

7. Bergamot and Geranium All-Natural Soap

What you need:

2.5 ounces lye

7.5 ounces water

20 ounces olive oil

10 drops bergamot essential oil

15 drops geranium essential oil

What to do:

Follow steps 1 to 7 of "Simple Olive Oil Soap".

Add the essential oils, and finish off with step 8 of "Simple Olive Oil Soap".

8. Rosemary Essential Soap

What you need:

2.5 ounces lye

7.5 ounces water

20 ounces olive oil

20 drops rosemary essential oil

What to do:

Do steps 1 to 7 of "Simple Olive Oil Soap".

Add rosemary essential oil, and proceed to step 8 of "Simple Olive Oil Soap".

9. Myrrh, Frankincense, and Rose Beauty Soap

What you need:

2.5 ounces lye

7.5 ounces water

20 ounces olive oil

5 drops myrrh essential oil

5 drops frankincense essential oil

7 drops rose essential oil

What to do:

Do steps 1 to 7 of "Simple Olive Oil Soap".

Add myrrh, frankincense, and rose essential oils to the mixture. Do step 8 of "Simple Olive Oil Soap".

10. Orange Sandalwood with Geranium

What you need:

2.5 ounces lye

7.5 ounces water

20 ounces olive oil

7 drops orange essential oil

8 drops geranium essential oil

10 drops sandalwood essential oil

2 tablespoons orange zest, grated

What to do:

Please see steps 1 to 7 of "Simple Olive Oil Soap".

Add essential oils and grated orange zest, and do process 8 of "Simple Olive Oil Soap".

11. Minty Basil Soap

What you need:

2.5 ounces lye

7.5 ounces water

20 ounces olive oil

6 drops basil essential oil

10 drops peppermint essential oil

1 1/2 tablespoons each of dried basil and mint, crushed

What to do:

Follow the same procedure 1 to 7 of "Simple Olive Oil Soap".

Add essential oils and herbs, and follow process 8 of "Simple Olive Oil Soap".

12. Robust Sandalwood and Patchouli

What you need:

2.5 ounces lye

7.5 ounces water

20 ounces olive oil

13 drops sandalwood essential oil

8 drops patchouli essential oil

What to do:

Visit "Simple Olive Oil Soap", and do steps 1 to 7.

Add the essential oils, and do step 8 of "Simple Olive Oil Soap" next.

Chapter 7: Novelty Soap Recipes

Novelty soaps not only clean, but can also turn a drab space (not just bathroom or sink) into a lively spot. Most of the recipes in this chapter use melt and pour method.

13. Swirl of Cucumber and Mint

What you need:

1 pound olive soap base, cubed

1 tablespoon each of English ivy and cucumber fragrance oil

4 drops peppermint essential oil

Light green mica

What to do:

1. Melt the soap base together with the fragrance oil.

2. Get two glass or stainless measuring cups, and pour the mixture evenly in the two measuring cups.

3. Add mica in one of the cups, and leave the other cup of mixture as it is.

4. When the mixture has cooled down a bit, begin pouring the content of each cup on the opposite sides of the soap mold and let the mixture meet half-way.

5. After transferring all of the mixture in the mold, get a stick and do a slight swirling motion in the soap. Do not overdo it. You only need to create a swirl pattern and not combine the color.

6. Put the soap mold in a cardboard box, and allow it to dry completely (see Chapter 5 "The Finishing").

14. Choco-Chip Soap

What you need:

1 pound coconut soap base, cubed

1 teaspoon cocoa powder or brown coloring (colorant)

1 pound cocoa butter

1 tablespoon chocolate fragrance oil

Soap molds that resemble a cookie

What to do:

1. Melt 3/4 of the soap base together with cocoa butter, cool for a bit and add the fragrance oil and some cocoa powder to give it a light brown color.

2. Melt the leftover soap base, add the colorant and make sure that it has a deeper shade of brown than the first batch.

3. Spread the darker batch on a plate lined with wax paper to hasten the hardening. When this batch turned hard, you need to cut them to resemble the chocolate chips. Line the chips at the bottom of the soap mold.

4. Pour the cooled bigger batch over the chips and topped with the remaining chocolate chips.

5. Put the soap mold in a box, and dry completely (see Chapter 5 "The Finishing").

15. Coffee Latte Soap

What you need:

1 pound coconut soap base, cubed

4 teaspoons lanolin

4 teaspoons gel of aloe vera

6 teaspoons coffee grounds

4 teaspoons whipping cream

15 drops coffee fragrance oil

15 drops vanilla fragrance oil

What to do:

1. Melt soap base in a double boiler, cool for a bit and add the fragrance oil.

2. Add the remaining ingredients and mix well.

3. Pour the mixture into the soap mold.

4. Put the soap mold in the cardboard box where it should be left to dry completely (see Chapter 5 "The Finishing").

16. Berry-Berry Smoothie Soap

What you need:

1 pound Shea butter soap base, cubed

2 tablespoons each of blueberry and raspberry fibers

3 tablespoons powdered goat milk dissolved in some of the soap mixture

1 teaspoon coconut oil

1/4 teaspoon pistachio fragrance oil

What to do:

Follow the steps in "Choco-Chip Soap".

17. Mocha Orange Bars

What you need:

1 pound coconut soap base, cubed

3 tablespoons cocoa butter

1 tablespoon coconut oil

1/4 cup ground coffee

Cocoa powder to serve as colorant

1 tablespoon orange essential oil

1 teaspoon cappuccino fragrance oil

1/4 teaspoon chocolate fragrance oil

What to do:

1. Combine the last three ingredients first and store in a dark colored vial and set aside.

2. Melt soap base and cocoa butter in a double boiler while stirring gently. Remove from heat when completely melted, and stir in coffee grounds and coconut oil.

3. Add coloring and the fragrance oil that you kept in the dark vial. Pour the mixture into the mold.

4. Keep the soap mold with mixture in the cardboard box, and cure it (see Chapter 5 "The Finishing").

Chapter 8: Guest Soap Recipes

Make you guests feel special with the soaps that you especially prepared for them.

18. Lots of Hearts

What you need:

1 pound coconut soap base, cubed

4 drops clove essential oil

1 drop each of cinnamon essential oil and buttercream fragrance oil

Deep red or burgundy coloring

Heart-shaped molds

What to do:

1. Melt soap base in a double boiler while stirring gently. Remove from heat when completely melted.

2. Add the essential oils, fragrance oil, and coloring.

3. Pour the mixture into the heart-shaped molds.

4. Place the soap mold in the cardboard box where it dries (see Chapter 5 "The Finishing").

19. Flower Power Soaps

What you need:

1 pound cocoa butter soap base, cubed

1 pound goat milk soap base, cubed

3 drops essential oil of your choice

2 drops fragrance oil of your choice

Mica coloring

What to do:

1. Melt soap base in a double boiler. Continue stirring gently. Remove from heat when all cubed soaps were melted.

2. Add the oils and coloring.

3. Pour the mixture into the flower-shaped molds.

4. Keep the soap mold in the box, and dry (see Chapter 5 "The Finishing").

20. Multi-Scented Guest Soap

What you need:

2 cups soap base, cubed

3 drops ginger root essential oil

3 drops orange essential oil

3 drops lemon essential oil

Gold, orange, and green coloring

You should also prepare:

3 small glass or stainless bowls

3 cookie cutters

3 trays

Parchment paper

What to do:

1. Melt soap base in a stainless pan, stir constantly.

2. Divide the melted soap into the three bowls.

3. Add gold coloring in the first bowl, stir. Add ginger essential oil in the same bowl, stir.

4. Add green coloring in the second bowl, stir. Add lemon essential oil in the same bowl, stir.

5. Add orange coloring in the third bowl, stir. Add orange essential oil in the same bowl, stir.

6. Get the trays and line each one with parchment paper. Pour each bowl of the soap mixture to each tray to come up with a thin layer of soap. Let the soap harden.

7. When the soap is hard enough (just right for cutting), cut it up using a cookie cutter (choose any shape you want).

8. Dry them a bit more by placing them inside the cardboard box.

21. Alphabet Soap

What you need:

1 bar of clear unscented soap base (about 8 ounces)

Coloring (your choice)

5 drops fragrance oil (your choice)

Small amount of white colored soap (unscented)

Alcohol in a spray bottle

You should also prepare:

Rectangular mold

Letter mold

Popsicle stick

Microwave

What to do:

1. Put the white soap in a microwavable bowl, and melt in the microwave for 25 seconds. Use a popsicle stick to stir a bit and repeat the process until melted.

2. Pour the melted soap into the letter mold, and freeze for 15 minutes or until it becomes solid. Unmold the letter.

3. Melt soap base using a double boiler.

4. Add in coloring followed by the fragrance oil. Pour the soap mixture into the rectangular mold. In case bubbles form, just spray it with alcohol.

5. Wait for the soap mixture to cool a bit and add the letter at the center (make sure that the soap mixture won't melt the letter.

6. Let it sit for a day before removing from the mold.

Chapter 9: Laundry Soap Recipes

In this chapter you will see simple recipes for laundry soap.

22. Natural Soap for Laundry

What you need:

Pure Castile bar soap (your choice of scent)

Washing soda

Borax

Baking soda (optional)

What to do:

1. Grate the bar soap or use a food processor to grind it finely.

2. Get a large bowl or container and follow this ratio: 1 part grated soap, 2 parts borax, 2 parts washing soda, and 2 to 3 teaspoons baking soda (you can omit this). Mix well.

3. Keep your homemade laundry soap in a closed container.

You can use 1/4 cup homemade laundry soap per load of laundry.

23. Liquid Laundry Soap

What you need:

Pure Castile bar soap (your choice of scent)

2 quarts water

1 cup Washing soda

1 cup Borax

4.5 gallons hot tap water

What to do:

1. Grate the bar soap using cheese grater or use a food processor to grind it finely.

2. Get a large casserole and add water and grated soap. Place the casserole over low heat while stirring to dissolve the soap.

3. Get a bucket that is large enough to contain the 4.5 gallon water. Stir in borax and washing soda and dissolve.

4. Pour in the soap mixture. Cover the bucket and leave it overnight.

5. Stir the mixture the following day and pour into gallon jugs to keep.

You can use 1 cup liquid laundry soap per load of laundry.

24. Liquid Laundry Soap Take 2

What you need:

1-200 gram olive oil soap

2 quarts water

100 grams washing soda

100 grams Borax

What to do:

1. Grate the bar soap, and get a large casserole. Put the water in the casserole and boil it over low heat.

2. Add the grated soap in the boiling water and stir until the soap has melted. Remove from heat. Make sure that the mixture has no lumps.

3. Get a bucket that is large enough to contain the mixture. Add in borax and washing soda, stir well.

4. Pour the soap mixture in the container and store away until needed.

25. Kitchen Soap Recipe

Here is kitchen soap recipe that you might want to try.

Easy Kitchen Soap

What you need:

1/2 cup liquid castile soap

1/8 cup water

4 drops lemon essential oil

1 teaspoon vinegar

What to do:

Mix everything well and store the mixture in a container or dish soap dispenser. Use it as you would a commercially produced liquid soap.

Chapter 10: Herbal, Germicidal, or Anti-bacterial Soap Recipes

Give these herbal, germicidal, or anti-bacterial soaps a try.

26. Cinnamon and Zesty Lemon Soap

What you need:

2.5 ounces lye

7.5 ounces water

20 ounces olive oil

10 drops cinnamon leaf essential oil

20 drops lemon essential oil

2 tablespoons lemon zest, grated

What to do:

1. Prepare all the things that you are going to use. Wear your protective gear while preparing your ingredients.

2. Place the water in a jug in the sink.

3. The room should be well-ventilated. Carefully add lye in the water, use a spoon when mixing. It is expected for the solution to get hot, be careful in handling lye.

4. Prepare your oil as you let the jug sit in the sink.

5. In a stainless pan, heat the olive oil over low fire. The temperature should be around 110°F. Turn off the stove.

6. Test the temperature of the lye solution; it should be almost the same as the temperature of the oil.

7. Add the lye solution to the oil, and gently mix them together using your stick blender until the mixture resembles a pancake batter.

8. Add the essential oils, and lemon zest. Mix well.

9. Pour the mixture into the soap mold with lining. Put the soap mold in a cardboard box to dry completely (visit Chapter 5 "The Finishing").

27. Lavender Basil Combo Soap

What you need:

2.5 ounces lye

7.5 ounces water

20 ounces olive oil

8 drops basil essential oil

12 drops lavender essential oil

2 tablespoons each of dried lavender flowers and basil, crushed

What to do:

Follow steps 1 to 7 of "Cinnamon and Zesty Lemon Soap".

Add basil and lavender essential oils to the mixture as well as the dried herbs.

Do step 9 of "Cinnamon and Zesty Lemon Soap".

28. Lavender, Jasmine, and Patchouli Herbal Soap

What you need:

2.5 ounces lye

7.5 ounces water

20 ounces olive oil

8 drops patchouli essential oil

12 drops jasmine essential oil

5 drops lavender essential oil

2 tablespoons dried lavender flowers, crushed

What to do:

Do steps 1 to 7 in "Cinnamon and Zesty Lemon Soap" recipe.

Add the essential oils and crushed flowers to the mixture, followed by step 9 of "Cinnamon and Zesty Lemon Soap".

Geranium, Jasmine, and Frankincense Soap

What you need:

2.5 ounces lye

7.5 ounces water

20 ounces olive oil

10 drops each of frankincense, geranium, and jasmine essential oil

What to do:

See steps 1 to 7 of "Cinnamon and Zesty Lemon Soap".

Add the essential oils to the mixture.

Proceed to step 9 of "Cinnamon and Zesty Lemon Soap".

29. Minty Foot Soap

What you need:

9 ounces soap base, cubed

3/4 teaspoon vitamin E oil

1/4 teaspoon each of blueberry and raspberry seeds

15 drops blueberry fragrance oil

15 drops raspberry fragrance oil

15 drops peppermint essential oil

What to do:

1. Melt soap base in a double boiler, cool for a bit and add the vitamin E.

2. Add in the remaining ingredients and combine well.

3. Pour the soap mixture into the mold.

4. Place the soap mold in the cardboard box to dry completely (visit Chapter 5 "The Finishing").

30. Your Favorite Herbal Soap

What you need:

8 ounces clear soap base, cubed

1/4 cup herb (rosemary, basil, calendula, lavender, or chamomile)

15 drops fragrance oil (your choice)

What to do:

Just follow the same steps as the previous recipe.

Chapter 11: Your Simple Recipe Guide in Concocting your Own Soap Blend

Are you ready to make your own blend? Always remember to wear your protective gear whenever you make your soap. Heed the warnings, follow the labels, and have fun.

In this chapter you will find simple recipe guide that you can use in concocting your own soap recipe. You can add other variations later if you are more confident in doing so.

You can also use the lye calculator that can be found online.

Your Recipe Guide A

Set first the amount of base oil in ounces that you want to work with.

For this recipe you need to follow this ratio for the base oils:

60% olive oil: 20% palm oil: 20% coconut oil

For your water, lye, and fragrance/essential oil:

32% water: 14% lye: 3% fragrance/essential oil

If you choose 50 ounces of base oil, then you will need these ingredients:

60% of that is 30 ounces olive oil

20% of that is 10 ounces palm oil

20% is 10 ounces coconut oil

32% is 16 ounces water

14% is 7 ounces lye

3% is 1.5 ounce fragrance/essential oil

Sample Recipe: Sweet Plumeria

You will need these: 30 ounces olive oil, 10 ounces palm oil, 10 ounces coconut oil, 16 ounces water, 7 ounces lye, 1.5 plumeria fragrance oil.

Do this:

1. Put your gear on, prepare the ingredients, and put the water in a jug and place it in the sink.

2. Work in a well-ventilated room. Carefully add lye in the water, and stir using a long-stemmed spoon.

3. Leave the jug in the sink, and get your stainless pan. Heat the base oils over low fire. Aim for 110°F. Turn off the heat.

4. Test if the temperature of the lye solution is anywhere near the temperature of the oil.

5. Add the lye solution to the oil, and mix them together carefully using stick blender. Mix until it resembles creamy custard.

6. Pour the soap mixture into the lined mold. Put the soap mold in a cardboard box, let it dry (visit Chapter 5 "The Finishing").

Your Recipe Guide B

You need to set first the amount of base oil in ounces that you want to work with.

For this recipe you need to follow this ratio for the base oils:

        80% olive oil: 10% palm oil: 10% coconut oil

You also need to determine the amount of water, lye, and fragrance/essential oil:

        32% water: 13.5% lye: 3% fragrance/essential oil

If you choose 25 ounces of base oil, then you will need these ingredients:

80% of that is 20 ounces olive oil

10% of that is 2.5 ounces palm oil

10% is 2.5 ounces coconut oil

32% is 8 ounces water

13.5% is 3.3 ounces lye

3% is .75 ounce fragrance/essential oil

Sample Recipe: Citrusy Soap

You will need these: 20 ounces olive oil, 2.5 ounces palm oil, 2.5 ounces coconut oil, 8 ounces water, 3.3 ounces lye, .75 ounce lime or orange fragrance oil or essential oil.

For the procedure, just follow the steps in "Sample Recipe: Sweet Plumeria".

Your Recipe Guide C

Set the amount of base oil in ounces that you need.

For this recipe, follow this ratio for the base oils:

        80% olive oil: 20% coconut oil

To set the amount of water, lye, and fragrance/essential oil:

        32% water: 13.8% lye: 4% fragrance/essential oil

If you choose 60 ounces of base oil, then you will need these ingredients:

80% of that is 48 ounces olive oil

20% is 12 ounces coconut oil

32% is 19.2 ounces water

13.8% is 8.25 ounces lye

4% is 2.4 ounces fragrance/essential oil

Sample Recipe: Simple Lemon Soap

You will need these: 48 ounces olive oil, 12 ounces coconut oil, 19.2 ounces water, 8.25 ounces lye, 2.4 ounces lemon fragrance oil or essential oil.

Just follow the instructions in "Sample Recipe: Sweet Plumeria" for the steps.

Your Recipe Guide D

It is important to set first the amount of base oil in ounces that you want for your project.

You need to follow this ratio for the base oils for this recipe:

        60% olive oil: 10% palm oil: 20% coconut oil: 10% canola oil

For the amount of water, lye, and fragrance/essential oil, follow this ratio:

32% water: 13.8% lye: 4% fragrance/essential oil

If you choose 75 ounces of base oil, then you will need these ingredients:

60% of that is 45 ounces olive oil

10% of that is 7.5 ounces palm oil

20% is 15 ounces coconut oil

10% is 7.5 ounces canola oil

32% is 24 ounces water

13.8% is 10.35 ounces lye

4% is 3 ounces fragrance/essential oil

Sample Recipe: Chamomile Soap

You will need these: 45 ounces olive oil, 7.5 ounces palm oil, 15 ounces coconut oil, 7.5 ounces canola oil, 24 ounces water, 10.35 ounces lye, 3 ounces chamomile essential oil.
Just follow the procedure in "Sample Recipe: Sweet Plumeria".

You can also use some of the already given recipes as guide in creating your own soap. Remember to read the labels and wear your protective gear when preparing your ingredients. The more you get to know the ingredients, the more you understand the kind of ingredients that will be able to help you create the kind of soap that you have in mind.

Conclusion

Thank you again for downloading this book!

Check out my other Best Selling Books Below!!

Preview From Best Selling Author Jessica Virna "Hormone Reset Diet"

Chapter 1: Hormonal Imbalance: The Root Cause of Weight Loss Problems

Have you ever wondered why none of the dietary programs you have tried really worked well for you? Do you still gain weight despite all your hard work in keeping yourself fit? Do you easily feel stressed out with simple things? If you answered "yes" to all these questions, then you have failed to address the real root cause of the problem—hormonal imbalance.

Here are some questions that you need to ask yourself first to help determine if you have imbalanced hormones or not:

- Do you usually feel a strong urge to eat sweets or carbs at 3pm?
- Do you find it difficult to get yourself out of bed in the morning?
- Do you easily get irritated even by simple things?
- Do have mood swings?
- Do you experience pre-menstrual syndrome every month?
- Do you have trouble getting a good night's sleep?
- Is your skin dull and dry?
- Do you have a belly fat that you can't seem to get rid of no matter what you do?

- Do you always feel bloated after every meal?

If your answer is "yes" to all of these questions, then your hormone levels are not balanced. Fortunately, this book was written specifically for you.

Women are more susceptible to problems pertaining to hormones. No matter how little we eat or how healthy our diet is, if it doesn't balance out hormonal misfires then the efforts will be wasted for nothing. There are different signs of hormonal imbalances and often women fail to recognize that.

- Pre-menstrual syndrome
- Irritability and mood swings over little things
- Extra weight hanging around the waist/belly area
- Excessive cravings for sugar
- Easily stressed out
- Difficulty sleeping
- Overwhelming feeling

Women need to know that hormones control nearly all aspects of losing weight. They affect your appetite, food cravings, fat storage, food patterns and even gut bacteria. This means that when there's hormonal imbalance, nothing will work out well for you unless you address this problem first. Eliminating junk foods and exercising regularly have always been the experts' advice on losing weight, but with hormones getting all fired up, losing weight will be difficult.

Click Here to Check out the Rest of "The Hormone Reset Diet" on Amazon

Or go to: **http://amzn.to/1HhshKh**

Preview Of "Anti Inflammatory Diet"

Chapter 1: What Is the Anti-Inflammatory Diet?

The Anti-Inflammatory Diet was originally invented by Dr. Weil, a nutritionist and diet expert. Often said to be almost similar to the Mediterranean Diet and the Zone Diet, but what makes it different is that it involves a lot of fish oil.

The Anti-Inflammatory Diet isn't just about protecting yourself from diseases—it's also about maintaining your ideal weight, too! When you're under this diet, you can expect that you'll easily be able to lose weight in a natural manner.

But what exactly is this about and what could Fish Oil, amongst others, do?

Benefits of Fish Oil

Fish Oil is a good source of Omega-3 Fatty Acids that could strengthen the overall condition of the mind, heart, and immune system in general. This is important because the human body cannot naturally produce Omega-3 Fatty Acids, and a lack of it would therefore bring forth a lot of deficiencies.

More so, one of the main reasons why you need Fish Oil and why the Anti-Inflammatory Diet is around is because it could protect you against Mitochondrial Dysfunction.

Mitochondrial Dysfunction

Mitochondrial Dysfunction results from a combination of erroneous stressors and aging that naturally bring forth a lot of diseases. When a person undergoes this, his cell walls are damaged—which therefore means that he easily becomes susceptible to a lot of negative medical conditions.

Another thing that happens is that free radicals make their way to the body, which then weakens cell membranes, and could bring about heightened levels of Uric Acid that could cause hypertension, slow metabolic rate, and a lot of heart problems.

When these things happen, Chronic Inflammation could take over the body.

Chronic Inflammation

As mentioned earlier, chronic inflammation could be the basis of a lot of dangerous diseases that could ruin the body—mentally, physically, and emotionally. What makes it really scary is the fact that there aren't concrete medical tests that could really check for Chronic Inflammation. Sure, there are cancer tests, heart disease tests, and more, but no one could be able to tell whether you're easily susceptible to these problems or not—and that's why in this case, prevention really proves to be better than cure.

Before you get to know what you should and shouldn't eat, it would be good to first know about what may cause Chronic Inflammation. There are 3 main categories for this, and these are:

1. Physical. This can come from one or more of the following:

Blunt or Penetrating Skin Injuries. It often happens when the injured person picks off scabs from his body.

Burns and Frostbite. These are two extreme effects of the weather, or of accidents that may cause a lot of pain and swelling for the afflicted person.

Debris, dirt, and splinters. Oftentimes, people neglect the way they experience these things and may sometimes be too lazy to take away unnecessary particles from their bodies, and thus, it leads to other diseases and worsening skin conditions.

Ionizing Radiation. There are certain diseases that can be cured by radiation, such as Cancer, but then again, it also has really adverse side effects, such as causing chronic inflammation.

Trauma. When someone gets into a terrible accident, swelling may be induced more and so he may suffer from chronic inflammation.

2. Biological, which is often related to reaction formations in the brain, and could be caused by the following:

Hypersensitivity. Auto-immune Disorders, and other complex immune diseases are often experienced by those who have hypersensitive immune systems.

Pathogenic Infection. Pathogens are microorganisms that may produce certain medical conditions, such as chickenpox, measles, mumps, smallpox, or worse, Ebola.

Stress. When you're stressed, you often experience unusual situations, such as having splotchy skin, feeling depressed, having the worst headaches, and extreme mood swings, which you may think are normal but may mean that certain parts of your body are already in too much pain.

3. Chemical, which are often brought forth by stressors that aren't natural to the body, such as:

Alcohol. Some people's lungs and bodies swell when they drink alcohol.

Irritants. Every person reacts different to irritants that may penetrate their body. Irritants are also called allergens—it could range from pollens, pet fur, legumes, dust mites, spores, or basically anything that makes a person itch, have splotches on the body, and have hard time breathing. You can always ask your doctor for an allergen test so you could determine which allergens you should be aware of.

Toxins. Unfortunately, there are a lot of toxins in the food that one eats and the many drinks around—so you really have to be vigilant and whenever you feel irritated or do not feel normal upon eating or drinking something, feel free to see a doctor already.

Other Factors

Moreover, certain conditions such as having elevated C Proteins, High SED Rate, High Homocystine Levels, Elevated Blood Pressure, and an inhibition of Monocytes could also trigger inflammation rate. It could also be brought upon by:

Age. Age is also a factor. More often than not, people who are in their 30's to 50's and older are more susceptible to this condition, because naturally, younger ones have healthier bodies and tougher immune systems. But then again, everyone's bodies are different so no matter how young you are, you still should not just dismiss this condition as something you won't experience at all. Mitochondrial dysfunction can happen to anyone.

Diet. Mostly, people who are overweight, suffering from Diabetes, and those who consume too much saturated fat are in danger of this.

Excess of Glucose. Glucose is tricky. When they're properly consumed by the body, they can be converted to energy, and the body can use it as its own fuel. But then, an excess of glucose has adverse effects to the body, which may destroy cells and bring forth chronic inflammation, especially when they're just accumulated in the bloodstream.

Low Sex Hormones. Unusual low levels of sex hormones not only kills one's sex life, it may also be the cause of inflammation, and bone breakage. It may also produce unusual symptoms of unease during menopause, as well.

Obesity. As mentioned, being overweight is a problem. When metabolism is affected, it already means that chronic inflammation is happening because the body can no longer secrete and store a lot of hormones and blood circulation is also affected, and thus, cells secrete more fat, which then leads to swelling of the body.

Sleeping Disorders. Pro-inflammatory muscles are elevated when one doesn't have a normal circadian rhythm, and when he almost always has a hard time going to sleep, which is also the result of the elevation of plasma in the body. It also happens to those who has narcolepsy and sleep apnea, too.

Smoking. Inflammation is produced by the thousands of chemicals contained in

Now, when your body gets affected by these things, you can expect that you'd suffer from certain diseases, such as Kawasaki Disease, heart ailments, stroke, Diabetes, Cancer, Chronic Lower Respiratory Disease, Alzheimer's Disease, Nephritis, and other Autoimmune Diseases.

So, what you have to do then is change your diet and improve your lifestyle—and it all starts with this book!

Click Here to Check out the Rest of "The Anti Inflammatory Diet" On Amazon

Or go to: **http://amzn.to/1Jf8k66**

Preview From Best Selling Author Jessica Virna "The Truth About Carbs"

Introduction

I want to thank you and congratulate you for downloading the book, *"The Truth About Carbs: Know How To Eat The Exact Amount Of Carbs To Melt Fat, Look Great Naked, And Stay Lean All Year."*

So many have tried countless dieting regimes — detox, vegan, Paleo, South Beach, etc. — but many had not yet met success in terms of weight loss and achieving a leaner, slimmer figure. What could be the problem? While the ultimate goal is to lose weight, some people have trouble losing *fat*. This book is aimed toward those dieters and anyone who wants to learn how to melt fat and stay lean, by focusing on the ever-elusive, ever-controversial *carbohydrates*.

This book will teach you the *truth* about carbs and how you can deal with this molecule. You don't have to *completely eliminate* carbs and say goodbye to your favorite food groups (never say goodbye to pastries or pasta!). You will learn how to eat carbs the proper way — for the benefit of your health and the success of your fat-loss endeavor.

Click here to check out the Rest of "The Truth About Carbs" on Amazon

Or go to: http://amzn.to/1RFykvc

Preview From Best Selling Author Jessica Virna "Essential Oils Therapy"

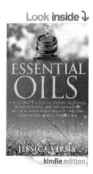

Benefits of Aromatherapy

There are various benefits of aromatherapy and possess different properties. Even if essential oils are good for first aid and relief, they are not enough to take the place of professional medication from licensed healthcare practitioners. Likewise, it is always good measure to have a person checked after providing first aid.

Essential oils can be unassuming but can have many versatile uses in a household. It pays to familiarize yourself with properties of essential oils so that you can act fast and know what needs to be done in case of emergencies.

Benefits

1. Improves skin
2. Helps digestion
3. Promotes sleep and relaxation
4. Natural first aid
5. Aromatherapy

Properties

1. Analgesic-some essential oils can relieve pain such as lavender, black pepper and bergamot.

2. Anesthetic-for emergencies, peppermint, clove, bay and eucalyptus can be used as an anaesthetic.

3. Antimicrobial-anise, bay, cajuput and benzoin along with black pepper have the ability to destroy or suppress microorganism and bacterial growth.

4. Antioxidant-essential oils can help remove damaging oxidizing agents in the body like ginger and benzoin.

5. Antiseptic-there are essential oils that can prevent decay like basil, bay, cedarwood, cinnamon, pine, sage, thyme and ylang ylang.

6. Antispasmodic-clove, cypress, garlic, thyme and basil essential oils can relive the nerves and reduce or prevent excessive muscular spasms and contractions.

7. Carminative-carminative properties mean that an essential oil has the ability to stimulate intestinal peristalsis, and relieve the expulsion of gas from the gastrointestinal tract. Such is the use of cinnamon, coriander, garlic, lemon, black pepper, basil and anise because they tend to introduce *heat* in the body.

8. Disinfectant-there are natural disinfectants in the organic world and the citrus essential oils are always dual purpose, like lemon and orange because of their acidic properties.

9. Stimulant-stimulants increase functional activity and energy in the body, which essential oils like bergamot, juniper, peppermint, jasmine and thyme can do.

10. Tonic- tonics tend to energize and strengthen the body like thyme, yarrow, black pepper, eucalyptus and cajuput.

Essential oils are more than just a good scent and home décor. There are many health benefits that can be derived from these natural wonders. Use your imagination and live a healthier lifestyle, you definitely deserve it.

Click Here to check out the Rest of "Essential Oils Therapy" on Amazon

Or Go to: http://amzn.to/1cUvAdI

Preview From Best Selling Author Jessica Virna "Weight Watchers"

Chapter 1. Weight Watchers and PointsPlus Value

The Weight Watchers® diet program is centered on food that is low in fat but high in fiber. Eat a lot of food within this selection in order to lose 1 to 2 pounds a day. There are times when you may crave for high fat muffins; the Weight Watcher recipes included in this cookbook has low fat and delicious muffins for you to prepare.

This diet program focuses on fruits, vegetables and protein that will enable you to increase your energy. Spend the energy at the gym to gain muscles instead of sitting on a couch the whole day.

Losing 10 lbs. in a week will not be difficult at all! The Weight Watchers® program now boasts of its new and improved PointsPlus values that will guide you to balance your food intake to lose weight. Based on a 1,000 calorie/day diet, you will learn how to eat a filling and balanced meal. Within the PointsPlus directives, you are allowed to consume 26 to 71 points in a day.

Keep in mind that you are not required to eat within the maximum limits that the point guide suggests. This is to give you a non-restrictive diet plan that will not leave you weak while in the process of losing weight.

Physical activity is needed to burn the extra calories that you have gained should you reach the maximum limits of the Weight Watchers® provisionary PointsPlus. In order for you to effectively lose weight, why not try to splurge more on fruits and vegetable? For you see, they have a PointsPlus value of 0. This way, you will feel full without having to think about the calories.

Among the Weight Watchers® dieters, this technique is called the filling technique. They eat designated food that does not add weight and calories. To bring the PointsPlus calorie tracker to a mathematical explanation, you simply would have to allocate points depending on your weight, height, activity level and age.

Aside from the PointsPlus® formula which can be calculated through a link in the website, there is also the ActivityPoints formula wherein you can check as to how many points you can include in your meal plan; based on the level of your physical activities. The more active you are, the higher your PointsPlus allocation is.

Keeping the weight off will not be a problem at all through the help of the Weight Watchers PointsPlus technique. This cookbook will show you the healthy way that the author chose to follow in order to lose 140 lbs.

Click Here to check out the Rest of "Weight Watchers Guide"

Or go to: **http://amzn.to/1G75fnI**

Preview From Best Selling Author Jessica Virna "Buddhism"

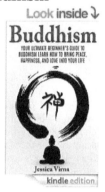

The First Noble Truth: Suffering

The enlightened Buddha realized that life is full of suffering. Whether one looks at his own life or at the world around him, this state is inescapable. The Buddha saw the world of suffering the moment he left the palace. In fact, the pre-conditions to fulfill the prophecy all pointed to different forms of suffering. Through the old man, he saw that everyone would eventually suffer of old age. One's former complexion may fade and wrinkles would surface. His strength would diminish; his capabilities would lessen.

The image of the sick man also portrayed the reality of people being prone to illnesses and diseases. Despite the joys of being healthy, this state wouldn't always be present. One's eyes may begin having difficulty seeing and other body parts may experience pain that wasn't formerly present. Moreover, death could strike anyone at any minute. In seeing the image of the funeral, Siddhartha saw that everyone would experience death.

For someone who was never exposed to pain, all these realities can be very overwhelming. From the moment a child is born until his death, pain would be present. However, these didn't cause Siddhartha to lock himself up in the palace. In fact, the words of the hermit even inspired him to discover more about suffering in the hopes of learning how to achieve happiness.

The first noble truth embraces the inevitability of suffering. Despite the joys and pleasures of life, pain would always appear. However, despite the negativity that this may indicate, the Buddha explains that these are normal. These should not be feared or hated. Rather, people must accept suffering and prepare for it.

Knowing Suffering

Suffering can come in two main forms. First, there is physical pain. This can be seen through harm inflicted on the body. Wounds, fractured legs, or even sickness are indicators of physical harm. Such suffering can be of varying degrees. They can last for as little as a few seconds to even an entire lifetime. However, while most people view suffering to be applicable only to the physical body, the Buddha clarified that this can also emerge in the spirit.

People experience various emotions. These include hate, anger, and greed. People can even feel depressed or lonely. Many of these are unhealthy and unwanted feelings that can affect one's health and disposition. The death of loved ones and other unfortunate events can also trigger such hardships and emotions. Failures and losses can also result to this painful sensation. While these emotions seem to be hidden and minor, they can cause worse effects than physical pain. In fact, they can even elevate the suffering caused by the physical body.

Although people want to experience as little pain as possible, it is clear that this would exist in everyday situations. Even the most minor nuances can trigger suffering. However, the Buddha teaches his followers that these are all natural. Instead of fearing or running away from such emotions, one should slowly and carefully learn to accept these. In fact, knowing suffering would be the key to eventually know happiness.

Of Suffering and Happiness

Although suffering is dominant in life, the Buddha also claims that joy and happiness can also be found simultaneously. Amidst the pain, there can be happiness in friendship, family, health, and other positive factors. These would depend on the perception of an individual. While there are times for suffering, there would also be times of happiness. Buddhists would claim that while both are part of life, these aren't necessarily present permanently. There is some form of balance which can be handled by individuals.

Knowing that suffering and happiness can coexist, the Buddhists proceed to explain that many people make the mistake of trying to escape suffering. They try to distract themselves by indulging in temporary pleasure. Drinking, gambling, and other habits are methods to forget about these unwanted feelings. In their attempt to block out sadness, loss, and grief, they try to delude themselves with pleasure. However, in reality, these wouldn't be effective and would just end up bringing more severe forms of pain and sadness. This would produce worse effects once the temporary happiness perishes. For example, if a person with a cold tries to cheer himself up by eating ice cream, this may just temporarily satisfy his taste buds. After a while, this would contribute to the worsening condition of his colds.

Applying the First Noble Truth

It is important to accept the first truth if one desires to be a step closer to knowing how to gain happiness and enlightenment. Although this teaching may be ancient, this is very applicable to this day and age.

1) **It's okay to be worried, but don't let it control your life.**
People may get the misconception that the first truth encourages them to stop worrying about bills, insurance, and other things. However, this is incorrect. Fear caused by possible suffering is normal. After all, it's an undesirable state to be in. One shouldn't become boastful and feel invincible to suffering. However, at the same time, one shouldn't let the emotions inflicted by suffering take control of his life. Instead of letting it dictate one's disposition, it should help strengthen one's morale and character. Yes, suffering can sometimes feel too unbearable. However, suffering will always be merely a state that can be overcome. Hence, there is a need to control one's emotions. In effect, he can live life more fully and strive to find happiness.

2) **Prepare for suffering. It will always be there.**
One shouldn't just offer himself to suffering. Of course, he should find ways to prepare for it or even prevent it from worsening. An individual can choose to plan ahead, ask help from friends, or other methods to cater to his needs. He doesn't have to face suffering unarmed.

3) **Be optimistic.**

Many people who experience suffering feel as if it indicates the end of the world. They may lose the will to work or even live. These thoughts won't be beneficial in one's pursuit of happiness. Suffering is perfectly normal. Though suffering may hinder a person to fulfill his goals or plans, this doesn't mean that suffering should take control of the rest of his life. One should still think positive amidst the pain he endures. This perhaps is the most effective way to combat such feelings.

4) **Be realistic.**
Suffering is very real and shouldn't be taken for granted. Hence, one should understand how it can affect his life. Knowing the implications of a certain form of suffering can be helpful as one responds to it. Understanding a certain health illness or consequences of not paying bills can all help the person experiencing problems.

For the Buddha, there is a need to focus on the realities of life. To achieve happiness, one must embrace whatever is happening in life. Distractions would be of temporary benefit but would be inevitably futile. Hence, as both happiness and suffering are both temporary, people must learn to live with these. This is the first step to achieving inner peace and enlightenment. Of course, it doesn't end there. The Buddha then proceeds to discuss the succeeding truths.

Click **Here** to check out the Rest of "BUDDHISM: Your Ultimate Beginner's Guide to Bring Peace, Happiness, and Enlightenment Into Your Daily Life" on Amazon

Or Go To: http://amzn.to/1QK7j8r

Preview of "The Mediterranean Diet"

Chapter 1 Benefits of the Mediterranean Diet

There is a renewed attention and enthusiasm about the Mediterranean diet in recent years. A lot of researches found out that the diet is rich in nuts, fresh vegetables and fruits, olive oil and fish, providing protection against serious illnesses. Aside from that, it also helps in maintaining a healthy weight.

More specific health benefits include:

Protection from Type 2 Diabetes

Traditional Mediterranean diet is rich in fiber. The fiber slows down the rate of digestion of carbohydrates. This way, the blood sugar levels do not quickly shoot up and just as rapidly drop. Type 2 diabetes develops from rapid sugar-insulin spikes that occur frequently.

Protects against stroke and heart diseases

Modern, average meals are high in processed food and red meat. All these contribute to increasing one's risk in developing stroke and cardiovascular diseases. All these food are highly discouraged in the Mediterranean diet. Also, red wine is more preferred than drinking hard liquor. Research studies showed that red wine contains beneficial compounds that provide protective effects on the heart and the cardiovascular system.

Reduced risk of developing Parkinson's disease

The diet provides a substantial amount of antioxidants obtained from the abundance of fresh fruits and vegetables. These antioxidants provide a protective effect on the cells against damage from oxidative stress. Parkinson's disease develops from the degeneration or destruction of the nerve cells. By taking more antioxidants, the cells will have better protection against destruction. This also helps reduce the risk of Parkinson's by as much as 50%.

Reduced risk of developing Alzheimer's disease

Research found that following a Mediterranean diet improves the body's lipid profile. It improves the levels of cholesterol in the blood and promotes better ration between LDL and HDL. Also, blood sugar levels are better regulated. All these improvements are believed by experts to help in reducing a person's risk for developing Alzheimer's disease.

Reduced risk for cancers

Healthier eating practices help in preventing several types of cancer. Increased fiber intake helps reduce colon cancers. Antioxidants from fresh fruits and vegetables help in strengthening the cells against damage and cancer formation. Vitamins and minerals help the body's organs to repair itself and recover faster and better, to prevent any cancer cells from developing within the damaged structures.

Improved musculoskeletal health

The diet is rich in natural vitamins, minerals and other essential nutrients that help keep the joints, muscle and the rest of the musculoskeletal system working well and free of pain. A study found that the nutrients supplied by the

Mediterranean diet helps in reducing the elderly's risk for muscle weakness and frailty symptoms related to advancement of age.

Longer life

Because of the reduced risk for diseases such as cancer and heart attack, a person has a 20% reduction in death risk. That is, those who follow the Mediterranean diet enjoy longer, healthier lives.

Weight loss

All these healthy eating practices help lose excess weight and maintain it within the healthy range. Numerous researches on obesity found that frequent sugar and insulin spikes promote fat accumulation in the body and slow down metabolism and fat burning. Unhealthy trans fats and saturated fats from the average diet are not utilized by the body and are stored as added fats. Also, the chemicals from food processing such as the preservatives, flavor enhancers and stabilizers all contribute to an imbalance in the body that promotes obesity. Take all these out and the body is able to return to its normal and efficient metabolism and fat control. The net result is losing excess weight.

[Click Here to Check out the Rest of "The Mediterranean Diet" on Amazon](http://amzn.to/1e1YtVA)

Or Go to: http://amzn.to/1e1YtVA

© Copyright 2014 by Angel Publishing Inc- All rights reserved.

This document is geared towards providing exact and reliable information in regards to the topic and issue covered. The publication is sold with the idea that the publisher is not required to render accounting, officially permitted, or otherwise, qualified services. If advice is necessary, legal or professional, a practiced individual in the profession should be ordered.

- From a Declaration of Principles which was accepted and approved equally by a Committee of the American Bar Association and a Committee of Publishers and Associations.

In no way is it legal to reproduce, duplicate, or transmit any part of this document in either electronic means or in printed format. Recording of this publication is strictly prohibited and any storage of this document is not allowed unless with written permission from the publisher. All rights reserved.

The information provided herein is stated to be truthful and consistent, in that any liability, in terms of inattention or otherwise, by any usage or abuse of any policies, processes, or directions contained within is the solitary and utter responsibility of the recipient reader. Under no circumstances will any legal responsibility or blame be held against the publisher for any reparation, damages, or monetary loss due to the information herein, either directly or indirectly.

Respective authors own all copyrights not held by the publisher.

The information herein is offered for informational purposes solely, and is universal as so. The presentation of the information is without contract or any type of guarantee assurance.

The trademarks that are used are without any consent, and the publication of the trademark is without permission or backing by the trademark owner. All trademarks and brands within this book are for clarifying purposes only and are the owned by the owners themselves, not affiliated with this document.

Made in United States
Troutdale, OR
01/29/2025

28461606R00037